A Different Measure of Moonlight

Poems

© 2003

Also by Toni Thomas:

Chosen

Fast as Lightening

Walking on Water

Blue Halo

Ace Raider of the Unfathomable Universe

You'll be Fast as Lightning Coveting my Painted Tail

Hotsy Totsy Ballroom

Love Adrift in the City of Stars

In the Pink Arms of the City

In the Kingdom of Longing

The Things We Don't Know

In the Boarding House for Unclaimed Girls

They Became Wing Perfect and Flew

Unburdened Kisses

Bandits Come and Remove Her Body in the Night

There is This

Here

The Smooth White Vanishing

Perishing in the Rain

A Different Measure of Moonlight

Poems

First published in 2023 by Annalese Press
134 Towngate
Netherthong
Holmfirth
West Yorkshire HD9 3XZ
England

Copyright © 2003 Toni Thomas

*All characters and situations appearing
in these pages are creatures of the imagination and in the
service of poetry.
Any resemblance to real persons
living or dead, is purely coincidental.*

All rights reserved. No part of this publication may be reproduced, stored, or transmitted in any form, or by any means electronic, mechanical or photocopying, recording or otherwise, without the express written permission of the publisher.

Cover design and layout by Peter Wadsworth
Girl with Pigtails, Amedeo Modigliani, 1918

British Library Cataloguing-in-Publication Data
A catalogue record for this book is available on request from the British Library.

ISBN 978-1-7394457-3-7

Lasting thanks to my children -
without their support and patience
this book would not be possible.

CONTENTS

Prologue

Innocence   1

Part One: *The Weight of Unpardonable Roses*

Blight   5
Rosita   7
The Will   10
Best Dresses   11
Vanya   13
Dear Amanda   16
City   17
Aunt Julia's Dress   19
Relations   21
Feisty Muriel   23
Invisible   25
Gardenias   27
Parting   29

Part Two: *The Consequential World*

Blue   35
Field Burning   37
Chickens   38
The Bridge Burning   41
House For Sale   45
The Weight of Things   47

Part Three: *The Excellence of Reitmann's Bakery*

Certainty	51
Cynthia	53
Yellow Yarn	56
Ivy	58
The Ring	60
Torched by Lightning	62
Sunday	64
Easter	66
Lizzy's Meditation Garden	69

Part Four: *Midnight Plagues*

Jonah Swallowed Up by the Whale	77
Cellophane	79
Crows	81
Black Rayon	82
Pleasures	84
Devotion	88

Part Five: *The Visitation*

The Climb	93
Taken	94
Gulls	96
Clemency	97
Remembering	98
With Child	100
The Recovery	102

Part Six: *Conjuring it New Again*

The Crank Box	107
Festival of the Fishes	109
Irene	112
In My Story	116
The Lesson	118
The Blue Ices	120
Mary Donahue	122
Levitation	126

Innocence

When the angels came
they were laden with heaviness
the lost fruit
weight of knowing so many
come to so little in this world

crept their roots around
my sawn wings
as if in flying I could be
made whole.

For the rest
it is history.

You came unclothed to my bed.
I closed my eyes
tasted indecency
your bare breasts
this aching.

PART ONE
The Weight of Unpardonable Roses

Blight

My father told me that when young girls
are called to heaven it's a blight
on the eyes of the world.

I wasn't sure I understood him back then
how the disappearance of someone
might steal the red from our souls
the way time can maul with an unforgiving hand.
Not till our neighbor's third daughter Madelaine
got yanked out of life by the blue pickup.
She was in the sixth grade, two up from mine.
I remember her hair that ran all the way down
to her belt loops.
Of the four girls in the Delaney family
everyone said she was the one most likely
to be chosen to wear a crown.

I remember in fifth grade class she got her
Virgin Mary poem pinned on the wall.
The nuns never yelled at her, asked her to stay detention
write 200 lines of the same sentence for saying a bad word
so I found it hard to believe she would be
forced to reach heaven faster than the rest.
Mama says the driver never saw her
kept weeping till the ambulance arrived
says she came out of nowhere, entered his path.
Madelaine Delaney dead at twelve years old.

After that I waited for the blight to come.
Sure enough it did.
The boys grew meaner, tucked rocks in their
snowballs for extra punch.
The children in my class started to fall.
First to pettiness and name calling
then snub nosed lunch room segregation

later to blatant shoving and incisors that grew
ungainly for their once soft lines.
As if heaven wore a traitor face.

Since Madelaine Delaney's innocence has gone missing
a vampire plagues midnight.
Plucked eyebrows have set in, fake eyelashes
weigh scales meant to tabulate heaven as
a boney wafer with no meat
clubs whose memberships have picket fences
all avoidance of gray.
Crushed ones with heads full of knowledge
unrooted feet.
If there is a blight on the world
it is a fire of locusts
insolence burning
my summer dress stabbed blue and dangling.

Rosita

Rosita Sanchez lived next door.
Her husband drove truck, guzzled beer
spat Cuban tobacco.
My mama never liked him
not since he kicked our cat one time
when she strayed into their yard.

I liked watching Rosita, the way her body moved
those flouncy dresses in hot pink, emerald trim.
Her spike heels that mirrored the sun.
She sometimes brought me crackerjacks
and once a pair of butterfly hair clips she says
someone left at the restaurant, never claimed.
Maybe she felt sorry for me always playing alone
or maybe we understood each other
those silences that mix with defeat.

My mother said it wasn't a restaurant she worked in
but a tavern—Salvador's Tavern on Hillside—and that
no decent girl would ever set foot in there.
When Rosita sent us leftover pizza slices one night
my mama threw them straight in the waste bin
warned me to not say a word.

Rosita's husband had greasy hair, was gone a lot.
Sometimes when he was away a red bandana
flapped on Rosita's side porch
didn't disappear until the day before he came back.
In summer, outside catching lightning bugs
I'd see an old blue Chevy cruise up and down the road.
My mother told me to shut my mouth
not go over there anymore.

In December I saw the heavy lights of a truck
pull up unexpected in front of their porch.

Her husband was back days early—heavy snow in the Rockies
and the red bandana he'd never seen still out there
waving blindly back and forth on the side porch.
It was 7p.m. My homework spread over the dining table
algebra—something I was never good at.
Suddenly it seemed like our house shook
we could hear things being smashed –a TV, radio
I looked out our left window and saw
a chair being hurled across the room
the wheels of a blue Chevy skidding down the wet road.
My mom told me to go to my room NOW.
I saw my dad grab his red check jacket
head out the front door, my mom shouting
No Dan, don't get yourself involved in this.
A few minutes later heard my dad calling the police
telling them to come quick
big ruckus next door, somebody likely to get hurt.
It didn't take long before the sirens arrived
neighbors came huddled in thick coats to have a look
and I could hear a policeman shouting
Open up! then kick in their door.

The husband doesn't live there anymore.
He's on parole and mama says there's a restraining order
so he'll never come back.
But Rosita, poor Rosita Sanchez.
None of us came fast enough to save her.
He tore a knife down the left cheek of her beautiful face.
It healed up. Sure. But she never looked the same.
Mama makes me stay away
says she brought the whole thing on herself
had a lesson to learn.

I remember Rosita Sanchez.
The crackerjacks she used to bring me

her gentle voice when she asked me about school
how my dolls were doing
her pink dresses before the soiled grey ones set in
the things some folks were born to do with
the sweet caress of their hands.

The Will

I will bury you with nothing but your cross he says.
She imagined herself naked in some grave
with ample thoughts, only her thin gold cross bleeding.
He would do that –
make a statement out of death
sexuality
as if her life was a placard
for his mind's treasons.

I will call you a serial murderer then.
A wolf who eats young girls
leaves their bones to rot in the wind.

He wanted her to sign on the dotted line.
About her death, that is.
In the eventuality of course.
He saw no reason to leave loopholes
snarl up the brain with indecisive.
It could be years before the plan ever
needed to be executed.

She streaked blue ink down her shirt.
Some say it was red blood.
You can never tell what a woman
will do with metal coat hangers
wound around her neck
and no one willing to stop
hear this other kind of singing.

Best Dresses

My mother, Mary Louisa, did not believe
the world would save her
not with its wide teeth
ferocious appetite for a woman's pink tongue.

To this end she tied a clothesline around midnight
kept her nicest dresses ready for better days.
I was eleven back then, watched her in the stained apron
sweep the yard's dust, roll bread sticks
wash load after load of hotel sheets that earned her pay.

May you never eat garbage from other people's backyard
she warned me.
I'd seen the callouses on her hands
proud way her one gold tooth pronounced itself in
stolen laughter
the chain she wore with the virgin's face.

Five years ago Aunt Truro married the rich American.
Now she never needs to mop floors
bake her own bread, stew tomatoes.
What are you saving your clothes for aunt would ask.
For the one who holds cicadas on his tongue
can sing the moon, my body, out of its longing
my mother would say as if she still had a dream in her.
Whoever this man was he never came.

My mother has grown old, her back stoops
she ices feet swollen the size of grapefruit
wants to believe I will never stray.
At eighteen I wander off to San Diego
meet my first girl

she wears dresses the color of mango
stockings with no runs
never tires of powdering her face
scanning the newspaper for carnival events
new restaurants.
I hide the dark bread on my tongue
secondhand trousers
pocket full of nothing I was raised on.

Tired mother
back on the porch I see you
unpacking a bone for our mangle of dog.
Where is the one you imagined could hoist
your waist to heaven with durable arms
where are those quiet seed buns
that lurk beneath the world's knife blades?
Where have I fled to with my treacherous hands
that hairpin the past
pin the night's longing to neon?

Vanya

Vanya had bleached blonde hair
that meant summer even in winter
deep arched feet, pearly long fingered hands.
I imagine she could have been
a concert pianist or dancer
if poverty had not stripped her mother
of all regality and reduced her simply to
the scrubber of other people's floors.

It was a bitter cold December.
Vanya came into Eddies in high heels
an unlined jacket with its flaps open
a scooped low dip neckline that invites wind.
We always wanted to know her secret—
how she could be out in the fiercest weather
with such flimsy clothes.
She said, *It's attitude. That's all it is.*
You just have to make your mind up
to stay toasty inside, then you do.
I was wearing wool and lots of it
red mittens, ear muffs, lined boots
could not convince myself
I was sauntering through the tropics
instead of just dreaming of them.

Eddie liked Vanya
thought she added a lot to the scenery
said her curves made the place a notch classier
brought in all the single guys for supper
who didn't want to go home.
Vanya was a good waitress.
I have to hand it to her.
On any given Friday night she topped out
Deb and Santiago's table tips by three to one.
Vanya, it's Saturday. What you up to later?

Old Sammie asks from the lunch counter
as Vanya passes.
*Taking a long hot soak honey
that's what I'm doing* replies Vanya
her hips sashaying between tables.

All the regulars wanted to know
who Vanya was dating, did she have
a steady, still live with her old
Russian moma in the Bolshoi district
when was her birthday, did she gravitate
toward roses or yellow carnations.
Nothing, I know nothing I'd tell them
and even if I did I wasn't going to let on
about her private life.
She was a figment of their longing
and I left her that way.

The truth is Vanya was not much for this world.
Three years into working at Eddie's
she dropped dead of liver failure
and if any of us saw it coming we never let on.
Her moma lived out in the rough neighborhood
past 57th and when Vanya was gone Eddie paid her rent
for three months like Vanya would have done
and the mother wept and blessed his hands
then we never heard about her again.

Vanya gone. It is hard to believe.
I've learned some tricks from her that help
make good tips but have no knack
nor the hips to make them like she did.
You're an ace creation! Eddie used to tell her
at the end of a shift when we were crowded into
a vinyl booth and somebody's idea of

a leftover tray of lasagna appeared.
Vanya would slip her nylon stocking feet
out of her spike heels
put two quarters into the jukebox
play *This Side of Heaven.*
Then she'd clear some chairs
drag Mickey, our stocky bus boy
up out of his seat and onto the floor.

I thought she'd always be here. At Eddies.
Making good tips, running sudsy bathwater
back at home on her Saturday nights
saving her pennies
eventually maybe meet a guy—tall, muscled
on furlough from the Marines who'd know
how to treat her right. He'd shop for her mother
repaint the apartment, be stationed in Hawaii
the Philippines, she'd always be getting exotic presents
in tissue layered boxes and the promise
they'd be together soon.

God knows, a comely young woman like Vanya
could have been a concert pianist
bosa nova dancer
if the cards had turned out different.
One thing's for sure— she had a knack
for making the customers feel special
delivered their coffee, steak, fries, dessert
just the way they liked it, calmed their heartburn
broken marriages, dead-end jobs
helped them walk away a little less lonely
less hungry then when they came in
with the sooth of her voice, hands, hips
that hot spot she kept tucked inside
the thin of her jacket.

Dear Amanda

There's a sliver in my heart nobody sees
wants to travel the wind, nest in a child's purple box.
I dream of not being inland anymore
claiming a house by the sea, back in Maine
where we squandered our kisses, money that summer
drove boy lovers crazy

dream of truck stops with rough edged waitresses
poky places - the postage size library
shy corner garden, cramped market
ballads with simple words that repeat and repeat
handhold knots willing to stay tree faithful
dangle our spindly legs over the river

dream of making love in the grass
soft hands, bird pecked kisses
the graffiti petaled springtime
back then —when the earth spoke lust
and I was young, foolish
stuffed everything I owned back into my car
willing to go anywhere
unfamiliar yet with concrete shoes
the way weight can buttress then bind
the impossible terror of how we lie to ourselves
anchor our past like butterflies
stick pinned to a black velvet mount
in the end become such very small rooms.

City

Fallopian tubes aren't something I feel
I need to discuss in public, nor hysterectomies
but my friend Alice needs to bare all.
I know about Tom's vasectomy three years ago
the chinks in their love life
viagra reports they've been studying
virtues of collagen, an eye lift
the unprotected sex her teenage daughter
Molly had two weeks ago that caused
an uproar at the dining room table
led to Alice's grandmother's Russian rose crystal dinner set
having to survive with one less bread plate, no gravy boat
two teacups with chipped lips.

Sometimes I want to move to the country.
Canby, maybe. But I don't want all the grey.
Don't want it to rain so much.
Canby where the barge still takes unhurried people
across the Willamette River for 75 cents a car
and the breakfast favorite at Chip's Lunch Counter
is ham, eggs, hash browns, biscuit, two coffee refills
for $3.75 and the *Special* sign never goes away.

You'd get bored living out there Alice tells me.
She knows the limp roses in my front yard
weed infested flower beds
plastic picnic cloth half torn off
takes me for a fair weather girl
especially months like this—dead winter
no snow on the ground
the city locked in grey hairnets with the rain slashing.
Tells me *you'd go stir crazy, bury yourself in the house all winter
or else live in your car, find excuses to drive back to the city.*
Of course I keep dreaming of my roots back in New England

the husband who before our marriage promised to go
later on our honeymoon rescinded with the excuse
I'd need to be the ace breadwinner with a class act job.

Alice claims sacrifice in a marriage can be good
learned at the couples retreat that giving in
is more than concession
makes for a prized peacock
your nuptial vows grown stronger.

Unlike me, she has a clear eyed faith
in the expertise that so called *professionals* can lend.
Alice gets things done—
chairs the PTA, works all year on the Rose Festival parade
attends yoga retreats in California
offers therapy part-time from a posh office
snaps up the best deals for her family's spring break
books a year ahead to get the double porch
corner cabin in August at Odell Lake.

When I talk to her I feel like such a disappointment
my hideous bobby pins, illegible datebook
so few answers to navigate this world by.

Aunt Julia's Dress

Kristin didn't have apricot tinted shoes, a silver bracelet.
It was Easter and she was convinced nothing
on her feet would match the dress.
The dress was a present from Aunt Julia
who hardly ever gave presents
therefore it was doubly special.

Come see me in the mirror, she invited everyone as she twirled.
We thought it fit fine, perhaps a bit too long, lacy
but not one of us was going to disrupt the illusion
of Cinderella look-alike she saw.

The problem is the shoes mama, she told me.
We need the right ones not to ruin the dress.
I said *Easter's tomorrow, honey. They will have to do.
The navy ones will look fine once I put a bit of polish on them.*

Kristin flung down the back zipper of her dress
tore it off her shoulders and stomped it on the floor.
*You can all celebrate Easter without me.
I'm not going out tomorrow with all the dumpy people in this house.
Everybody already says my parents are dorks
and you look porky with too much weight.*

Some things are not kind or sensitive in this world.
No one made Kristin scour out her mouth.
The next day, Easter morning, she kicked, dragged herself
out of the house without one good word to say
except how she hated me and never wanted to wear
Aunt Julia's stupid dress anyway

which she didn't, she wore her dark brown one
with the yellow collar, said it matched her mood
and the house she lives in.

After that I felt that nothing fit me right
not my clothes getting skin tight around the hips
or my job strapped to a computer terminal
not our cramped house, crabby daughter
the man I married with his good intentions
who'd probably stay at the mill for another twenty years.
All the empty American desires I could see
would keep burning and burning and burning
our lives away.

Relations

They never talk to each other
not since his aunt died.
She spent years being looked after by them
till the last year of her life when she went
with her daughter, Vinnie
and the will mysteriously changed.
Vinnie took over the two farmhouses, seventy acres.
His father, her brother, might have wanted things different
but his father died twenty years earlier of throat cancer.

The whole homestead would be sealed in Vinnie's name
fall eventually into the hands of her only son
the New York artist who came out summers, slept in the barn
when the properties were rented
re-charged the battery on his old Harley
bombed through fields at night with his headlamp burning.

I was just a renter back then.
Didn't like feuds, animosities
that keep Christmas cards from coming
erect fences with double padlocks
wire posts where an open dirt road used to be.

Even though they built a compact chalet
on the parcel of land a mile down the gravel road
she never knew her nephew's family.
A decent guy, he built up an auto repair business
had two brothers working for him
a three week backlog to book in your car.
Replaced my brakes once, did a first class job.
They raised four children in that compact house.
The wife, a hairdresser, trim and friendly
who brought us a plate of holiday cookies one year
had us over for hot cocoa.

Their middle child had been accepted at Vassar
to study International Relations
and for the first time ever the parents told me
how they'd managed to overcome their fear of flying
board a plane in late August for the East Coast
to get her settled into her dorm.

Vinnie clear-cut a portion of the old growth
to pay her inheritance tax
put both properties in the hands of a rental company
two years ago when she got tired of dealing with
busted water heaters, frozen well pumps.
Leased out the field in front of our rental
to a local farmer who grows timothy
gets herself an agricultural tax break.
She is a painter married to a neuroscientist/ academic
comes back every summer
with silk-screened bandanas wrapped over her head.
Has an auto agency come out, charge the battery
of her old Ford truck, stays a month in the spare room
of the antique farmhouse rental up the road from us.
Tells me *read Stendhal*, checks the upkeep of both houses
the state of her parlor stoves, heirloom furniture.
In March she sent me a postcard from Florida
about a gallery retrospective of her work.

Vinnie's nephew still works at his auto garage
the decent life he's paved in a small town
amid the Coast Range cedars and solitude.
Place that is, was, will always be his only home.

Feisty Muriel

It never surprised me she had a younger man for a suitor
pampered him in small ways with her pasta, potato casseroles
wore her curvy body in dresses that clung to her waist
spewed blood red petals over the grey of winter
her auburn curls bouncing.
It was something about the way she entered a pub
talked passionate about the Thatcher cuts, miner's strike.
Back then she smoked cigars, imported ones
now that her two boys were grown
lived alone in that handsome old three story house in Surrey
that was crumbling slowly year by year since the hard divorce
since the money her accountant ex-husband squirreled away
in favor of his new girlfriend.
Her two young sons never saw him after that
grew up to have a father who was a distant stranger.
She told me he was good at looking penniless
and she had stopped trying to fight him
worked an ordinary office job up the road in Woking
took the bus everywhere
at night ate grilled sausage on a tray by the portable heater
paid a retired gardener to still come and prune the hedges
weed her succulent flower beds, manage the lawn.

It never surprised me that my British first husband's mother
kept the encumbrance of briars firmly away from her door.
She was too sexy, smart, armed with good cheer to let
the day slip away, glue herself to a box full of disappointments
planned winter trips to Portugal, Italy, Spain even after
her young, shy vegetarian boyfriend stopped coming over
found someone else, continued to go off, alone now
on her sunbaked annual excursions.
At 52 learned to drive, bought a 1972 Morris Mini
took herself off to Devon

or down to the local Three Lion's Pub on weekends where
her friend Maddie from South Africa told riotous stories
kept her pub owner husband, Billie
from falling apart with scotch.

I remember my first husband's mother
the eight years I lived in England, her beautiful son
I took away to the other side of the world.
The marriage didn't last.
But that was long ago.
Muriel may be dead by now.
I was too young
didn't know how to be in a marriage
didn't know who I was.
Still it remains—the raw edge of their laughter
desire to seize every moment
this remorse of mine beyond weeping.

Invisible

I don't want her to have a drinking problem
to disappear in the middle of the afternoon
come back petulant, ready to contest
the first thing I say about the perils of sugar
the new administration's tax cuts
my son's tutoring needs for dyslexia
whether galactic warfare on the big screen is really
as much innocent modern day fairy tale as she thinks.

After all she is an accomplished woman.
My husband has always lauded her for that.
A chemist. A Ph.D. who has managed a home
professional career, two children
till they were sent off finally to boarding school at 13.

Sadly two women, yet we don't ever get close.
Even at the Christmas church service
her lips cannot seem to rise to meet the singing.
I don't know how to find the breeze in the closed window.
She comes, takes over the kitchen, her men.
Christmas has always been her kind of affair.
All the elaborate cookies, precise lunches
Polish entrees just as she wants them.
But the holiness of the season no longer finds me.
Only the sobriety, the endless dishes
her sudden loss of appetite in the middle of
the exquisitely laid table.
We have to plastic bag her meals for later when she can't eat.
The long nap times, endless car trips to the grocery store
the cheap sherry in big bottles her husband and son
pretend not to see.

What surprises me is how invisible things can be
no slurred words, erratic sleep times
only the talk of gourmet food, next meal, accomplishments.

Her husband does what she commands.
Her son does what she asks.
I move to the corner of the room
wash dishes that are inspected
stay out of the way
grow a sudden rash on my face
escape to drop off my daughter
for a sleepover

don't want her to have a drinking problem
closed window I can't reach
don't want everyone to pretend
never confront her, get help.
She's always seemed so powerful
intellectually impeccable, in control
conscientious in the absolute merit
resolute grip of her ways.

Gardenias

Some say her life was too tropical for here
but I saw nothing tropical about it
she was always fighting off food frenzies
stuffing kids' lunch boxes
banging pots and pans to signal
the dinner meal's baneful.

They say it was the red gardenias
on that dress she always wore
the torn magazine articles of islands
that signaled her exile and demise
the way she imagined herself beachcombing
in a midriff top with no flab
all the delusions that set in.
The truth is they never went on an exotic vacation
never managed to catch up on overdue bills
spare the tax return
let a nuanced sun away from
the Northwest grey enter.

It was a shame some said.
She used to be such a comely girl
so many stories and fairytales inked up her arm
and the future her mother had planned for her.
It was the time going to college in Rio that killed it
one of the neighbor women said.
Got too high minded and she forgot her roots.
Sooner or later she had to be yanked back down
to earth again.
Still they said her life was too tropical for here.
In Spring she dug out her web chair
planted it in the middle of the front lawn.
Put out bird baths, feeders, gnomes

a bust of Aphrodite
rammed the metal legs of her neon flamingo
into the hard earth and sat.
Woman in red gardenias seated in paradise.
Out there all hours waiting for the moon to rise
clear above the rooftops
her husband's sensible.

The children grew weary of calling her in
for bath time, jammies, a goodnight kiss
eventually rolled themselves up in blankets
kept her company on the front lawn.
The three of them wielding flashlights
circles of shine in the dark
enough to lure the stars
assure the moon is watching.

Parting

Come the gray days of February
she plastered rhinestone clips to her hair
burnt toast, pasta
shrank from the kitchen
no longer believed anybody could love her
not after the great sex wore thin
and she started wearing those tattered nighties
not when she sat for hours hunched up
on the fire escape out the bedroom window
sucking coffee, cigarettes, seeding her hands
in the blue ink from those cheap pens.

It surprised her friends when she married him.
She said even though he'd been a business major
he spoke to the oranges, apples in the produce section
of the co-op where he worked, won her over.

Maybe it started with the abortion.
He didn't want that child, scraped up the money.
Said they had to do it, newly married
just moved into a shoebox apartment in hip Boulder
his new human resources job barely under way.
She --demoralized in line with all those Ph.D.'s
willing to wash dishes, wait tables
just to keep the Flatirons out their back door.
No job, no money, a floundering marriage, her first pregnancy.
She missed her own apartment, its aerial view, fire escape
her blue pens, god writing up and down her arm in the dark.

It took a year for them to become foreign to each other.
Three more months, two states, and three living places
before he walked out the door with his bags, a petite little lady
he'd met at a credit union convention who knew how to be
a team player and already had kids.
On the verge of divorce, just before Christmas

she moved into the old mansion in northwest Portland.
Rented a small room with light on three sides, French doors
a small side deck where her black spaniel could play
she could sit in a web chair, read student papers
look out at the rooftops' bleeding.

He never said out loud she was delinquent
too pie eyed to see the world straight.
She never promised him a perfect life
a woman willing to sacrifice her odd devotions
at the altar of matrimony
a slim girl
without cake batter clamoring
or those emerald shoes
so loose on her winged feet
as if in bystanding the world
she knew it would part for her.

PART TWO

The Consequential World

Blue

Nearly no hair on my head
just enough to keep cold drafts at bay.
And how many seasons are left
how many cat lives
broken vows, grand schemes
warm lit places, lust?
And maybe lust isn't half bad
after the endless months handling grade sheets
lesson plans, the hard fist of a Northwest winter.

I remember her, don't want to
product of a hot day
thin dress with crisscrossed straps
lips splashed in coral.

She knew how to whisper
take my body to islands
with windswept trees
move up and down my rocky coast
without stealing.
Had found a room inside herself
soft, widely lit.

It was long ago.
I wasn't veiled back then
wasn't the color of disillusion
the birds' lost mating.

And I remember my mother
when I was eight, maybe ten—
and most families had a father
remember her blood shot eyes
her dough in the bowl punched down

before it would rise into
a hard golden crust for me

remember her leathery sacrifices, two jobs
no nonsense blue apron
strict prayers
the church pew she dragged me to on Sundays
with its own brand of redemption
remember my words pared down
the wild crop of my hair burning.

Field Burning

He no longer remembers August
back in the farmhouse
the smoke from the fields' burning
the last of the season's peaches
on the farm up past Manning
the way they defied the width of his hands
huge as softballs and how the juice
came pouring down his chin, his neck
trickled into those secret places.

He may never get well again.
His asthma has turned into people jitters
till he never comes out of the house
forgets the smell of his grandmother's orchard
forgets the name of his dog
how to water the geranium
almost forgets his name too
till those men in white coats threaten to save
drag him to the place of colored pills.

Now he sits by the picture window all day
calm as crushed lightning.
But what will happen to the black dog?
He's big, seven years old
too old to be orphaned away.

Chickens

When Mrs. Moynihan's last chicken died in her backyard
everybody thought it was heat stroke
and not from its shrunken wing.
Mrs. Moynihan mourned for days after that
sent her deaf cousin away
only came out to collect the grocery bags
Saul from Campbell's Market delivered.
My mama said it was a shame about the dead chicken
but a sin the way she was carrying on over it
what with blood being shed
in a lot of other parts of the world.

For Easter Sunday I get to wear my new straw hat
with the fake pink rose
my mama will buff my little brother's buck shoes
till the sun shines on their face.
Papa has agreed to be dragged to church service
in exchange for the baked ham, scalloped potatoes
applesauce suzies my mama has promised.

Leland two doors down always has mud on his shoes
looks like nobody washes him
runs errands for Mrs. Moynihan, yanks weeds
rakes last season's leaf fall
polishes her living room windows come Spring
when the birds start nesting
in that big old maple we all want to climb.

Mrs. Moynihan never had a son, never married
watched after her mother who became pretty crabby
with back pain the last year
keeps company with her deaf cousin Louie
now that his only brother has moved away.

Easter is coming late this year but so is the rain
our daffodils drowning

the pathway my mother's dug in petunias
a mud soup our rubber boots swish in.

In the midst of Good Friday, thick sugar glaze
nearly burying the faces of our hot cross buns
my mother dusting the side table
knickknacks, her men's shoes
it is hard to remember there was ever a brood
of noisy chickens in Mrs. Moynihan's back yard.
They started dying slowly one by one over a year ago.
Old Gretel was the last one to go.
Mrs. Mohanihan gave her that name
claimed *she's stupid enough to take poisonous apples
from a stranger but loyal just the same.*

Mrs. Moynihan never shows up for Easter church service.
It's a long affair and I can see my papa fidget
impatient for the plates of baked ham to arrive.
Mama says we ought to bring over some soda bread
to Mrs. Moynihan, check on her.
You must come over, dear my mother suggests.
*We're having ham and all the fixings in about an hour's time
and I've already set a place for you at the table.*
Mrs. Moynihan's eyes are pink.
*Thanks, Dinny, but I can't. Gretel wouldn't want it.
Not yet three days cold in the grave and me going off feasting.
No. She's been with me a long time, was the only one left.*

It took another four weeks for Mrs. Moynihan
to regularly come back out the front door
tend her tulips, sweep porch, sit in the green rocker
with her binoculars watching swallows
nest building a storm up in her tree.
Cousin Louie has come back, is living upstairs again

in the left corner bedroom.
The Quilters Show is due to begin late May.
I never see Leland clean and shine the windows anymore
or sweep up her yard debris.
My friend Alice says his father drinks too much
and that's why he's got dirty nails, never gets any new shoes.
His mother died years ago of pneumonia when he was three.
But my guess is that it's because of all the chickens
gone missing
how he can no longer hope to bring home that magical egg
the one in the story books that sets a child free.
He once told me he was always looking for an egg
so strong, so beautiful it could outlast the rain.

But Billy Brennan from our third grade class
likes to play detective, claims he's got the real story
says he saw Leland through the fence mixing
black goop from a bottle into the chicken feed
that he killed them in secret one by one.
Maybe Leland couldn't bear Mrs. Moynihan
loving those chickens more than him
not when love is so scarce in this world
counts for more than those stupid spare eggs
more than the nests she gazes at for hours in her tree.

The Bridge Burning

When George Basconi set the Soco Bridge on fire
nobody had much patience with him.
He'd been to detention center, three foster homes
folks felt he'd had his fair share of chances.
He's just warped 60-year-old Franny Tucker next door said.
Her son had been in the Marines, came back with two medals.
Everybody knew that.

George was fourteen, walked with slouched shoulders
always seemed to be peering at the ground
searching for ants, free coins
instead of saying *hello* like everybody else.

Our town, Randall, is a small place
it's hard to be invisible here
everybody knows your report card
the fibromyalgia your mom is fighting
the fancy new gas barbecue in the Fletcher's backyard.
The downtown Sears pretends to be doing o.k.
but you can't help but notice it's surrounded
by boarded up businesses and since the tannery and
the wool works closed the service industry and construction
jobs down by Quincy where the condo craze is booming
seems about all that's left to us.
The high school seniors talk about getting out
moving to Quincy for a job or else
the two year community college or if they're really lucky
finding a loan ticket to the state university.

If George Basconi had plans like that nobody knew it.
He was no talker. When Cleopatra Pauley (who was really
Mavis but she couldn't stand it, so she wed herself
to a more exotic name)
chirped up that George's still life drawing in art class
of a grape and cheese platter was so accurate
she could almost taste it

the rest of us had to agree.
He had a way with shading fruit and capturing the lines
of junked trucks, broken down alleys, glass bottles
that any one of us might have envied if it much mattered.

At recess he sometimes shot baskets, mostly played alone
got the public assistance lunch
with plastic wrap, ageless apples.
Sally J. from my math class said she heard he was left
on a doorstep by his mom when he was seven months old
none of his foster placements ever turned out.
The one he is in now has seven kids.
She told me he never smiles
because he has black crud on his teeth.
Sally said her mom told her it only happens
to kids who never brush or floss, get dental checkups
take care of their mouth properly like the rest of us do.

It was on February 26th, just after nightfall
when the fire broke out.
Nobody could hear the TV once the sirens started whirling.
My dad put his jacket on
headed out the door to see what was going on
said afterwards that George Basconi was just sitting there
lumped up in a heap, next to three empty kerosene cans
a box of matchsticks.
Wouldn't say a word when the cops questioned him.
Dad says they cuffed him and booked him on the spot.
That was over four years ago.
I hear that George is still waiting final sentencing.
Rumor has it he's had two public defense attorneys

that didn't mount up much of a case
and one fell asleep at the trial.

I think of him sometimes.
His teeth. How kids laughed at his grammar when Mr. Jacobs
made him write something in class up on the board
the way he pitched those baskets out in the school yard
rarely ever aced one, me wishing he'd triumph over the net
show those other snot nosed kids
who thought they knew it all
that even someone with a sketchy hard past
nothing special waiting inside their door
can still find some small corner of happiness
on a grimy basketball court
with a bunch of hard-eyed kids judging.

I left Randall when I was 18.
The bridge was eventually rebuilt with state funds.
There's a new B&B some hopeful lady
from California opened and five modular units
behind the gym where the ninth grade classrooms are.
When I come back from college on spring break
or summer vacations they always say
what a *bad egg* George Basconi was.
Funny how, even years later, the bridge burning
still gives the town something to talk about.
Even at the Plastic Parts Factory in Hale
where I do swing shift in summer to earn college cash
the workers have no patience for anyone
not willing to do bags of overtime
sweat blood for a 25 cent raise
claim that everybody in this country gets the same fair shake

swipe at the carousel ring
just that some of us like George Basconi
commit arson, really blow it.

At break time in the back room with no windows
cigarette smoke consumes the air.
The guys here don't have much patience
for the likes of George B.
After all, they kick butt all their lives
to keep their truck wheels turning
a decent roof over their head, kids in school clothing.
The Plastic Parts Factory.
Even George might end up here on a second chance
if he gets parole someday.

House For Sale

It was grim to hear she died like that
alone with just the radiators hissing
three days and three nights they reckon
her battle with death fought on swollen knees
the empty aluminum soup cans on her counter listening
not even one picture or poster of the green earth
to cheer up those walls.

My older sister Carrie says she brought it all on herself
for months had forgotten her friends
refused to return phone calls.
After all, we all have busy lives my sister reminds me.
She can't keep expecting us to drop everything
and drive over to see her regular
when she barely even answers her door.

It was grim to hear Elinore died like that.
Eighty two and diabetic with all three of us living out of state.
My sister says social security covered her meds.
That she had a pension. The house was paid up.
There was just no reason she should have stopped eating
let herself go.
Her younger brother even drove seven hours to drop off
a black calico kitten called Ginger last autumn.

After the funeral the house needed some fixing up
before we could sell it.
Two of us came from out of state
repaired the torn fence, had a new oil furnace put in
geraniums stuck in pots, wicker chairs placed on the porch.
While painting the trim on the outside, I began recounting
to my sister, Lizzie, the newspaper article I'd seen
in the Seattle Times about a woman who gets buried alive
behind a brick wall.
Being a psychologist I tend to be fascinated with such things.
Lizzie descended the ladder, squeamish

45

stopped me mid-sentence
I don't want to hear that morbid stuff, Dan
talk to me about life, she says
about sailing around Puget Sound in summer
the way even this old house, its slumped lines
looks chipper now that we're giving it a new coat of paint.

I drew in a quiet breath
grew intent on the even stroke of my paint work
the inoffensive blue color of it
the way life doesn't always turn out
as you originally planned
how we dig graveyards
try hard to bury the rain.

The Weight of Things

It is a consequential world my father tells me
every action sits like a sledge hammer
bearing the weight of your fate.
And I remember as a five year old playing alone
the consequences of speaking up
my father's bright red hand slicing.

I remember cramped rooms, too many sick days
their marriage made of three jobs
sewn shut kisses
my mother climbing the walls, coloring them black
with her stumped down version of paradise.
She chain lit the night away.
And I remember the consequences
of too much name calling
the marooned world in my bed
lost lovers
way I walked away when I couldn't accept
what might become a small life
neat identical houses with my wrist bleeding.

Something, someone kept ushering me into the open field
the no name trellis of roses
pale alleys where plans fall like bowling pins
and nothing seems sensible or certain.

It is a consequential world my father told me.
Now all my hours an antique glass ball waits
washes my world in drifts of snow.

PART THREE
The Excellence of Reitmann's Bakery

Certainty

My doll Marguerite has big feet, that's why my friend Nancy
never likes playing with her. But I say she has purple shoes
how many dolls do you know with purple shoes on?
It makes no difference.
Nancy has her mind made up on most matters -
like which family on the block has the meanest dad
what season brings the most chocolate
the best dress color for smart girls with blonde hair.

It gets annoying at times being with someone who
navigates with such a firm voice
knows for sure where the stars come from
that toys only by their own choice turn deadened
the world is no wobbly vessel, except for the cursed.

But we both agree on the excellence of Reitmann's Bakery
their chocolate éclairs with whipped cream inside
although Nancy says I never eat mine right.
She asks me why I devour it instead of prying
the white petals slow one by one like she does.
Because I don't want it to disappear before I eat it.
Things don't disappear like that she replies.
A dog could nab it I explain *a hungry bee, stone thrown from the sky.*
Nancy rolls her eyes, keeps prying the petals of cream
loose with her delicate tongue.
But some things aren't delicate in this world.
Get snatched up like the litter of kittens under the porch
at my cousin's bungalow.
My cousin says the mama cat whines
roams up and down fence lines
prowls the space under the porch
desperate to recover them.

I say things happen like that.
You just have no faith in the world Nancy tells me.
She can do anything.

Roller skate down the steepest hill
and stop before the cars hit her
talk Mrs. Grunnidge, our third grade teacher, into going
on yet another field trip because the last one turned out
disastrous at the Pumpkin Patch with too much rain
get her mama to double her allowance for the doll
up at Percy's Toy Store we spotted a month ago
with jogging clothes and an all-terrain vehicle
that lets you go anywhere without getting stuck.

I offer to help if she can't finish her éclair.
We set my dolls up outside next to the basement wall.
Marguerite looks cold with her bare shoulders and scant skirt.
Nancy tells me it's good for her.
Builds up her body metabolism so she can
burn more fat calories without needing to eat less.
I ask *Where'd you hear this from?*
My mom. She knows lots of secrets for staying slim.
Never wears a jacket unless she has to
runs with a sports bra and shorts even in winter.
I like cardigans. Image my doll Marguerite in white lamb's wool
with pearl buttons, a pint size version of rabbit slippers
tucked on her feet.
Her shoulders with no goose bumps
nuzzled up on some window seat
inventing the world new as fresh snow
watching the white flecks disappear slow, delicate
willingly where they land.

Cynthia

Cynthia loved cats, I remember
and the crowbars and wrenches
her father asked her to hand him.
She always had greasy hands
a snotty way of diagnosing other folk's car problems
marriage ailments, bruised heart.

When I was ten she bought me a Woolworth's valentine
a big heart shaped red box of candies
with a plastic yellow rose attached to the top.
I wasn't sure what to make of it.
Already I harbored fantasies
of secret male admirers—
Jimmy Stein in the fourth grade class who slicked
his hair back too much but knew all the presidents
could recite the poem about red wheelbarrows.
Byron with the freckled face who could lop
off so many baskets in the net at recess
that everybody respected him.
Of course nobody noticed me.
Chubby, labeled teacher's pet
baby who cried and got sent home after
each attack of merciless teasing.

The candies were chewy with a milk chocolate coating.
I liked them better than the ones with dark chocolate
broke the skin on five or six to find the ones filled with cherry.
You're going to get fat my mother said.
Cynthia said she thought I looked just fine the way I was
like the Venus de Milo she'd seen a picture of
in some magazine and cut out and taped to her wall.

That summer Cynthia started to watch our house more.
Ran over when I got my bike out
and we'd cycle to the school playground together.

She had oversized hands, sandals that flapped
because they were too big
hardly ever got the car grease out from under her nails.

What do you want to do with your life? She'd ask me.
Don't know. Maybe get out of here. See the world.
Glue myself to books. Write a great novel someday.
She started climbing the monkey bars.
Why don't you stay here like me.
Help learn my dad's business.
We could become partners with him someday.
We'll set up a garage over at Queens Village
and everybody will book in there for repairs.
That would be nice for him I said.
No. For you and me too.

I changed the subject.
Cynthia let's bike past the bakery
see what they have in the window.
Cynthia wasn't interested.
Do you have any change? I asked.
No. Besides you don't need the sugar she burst out.
What are you saying? Are you telling me I'm fat?
You said it, not me.
I was trying to figure out where all this was coming from.
How we'd gone from a bike ride and the monkey bars
to an indictment of my body shape.
I've got to get back I tell her.
We hardly speak all the way.

Months pass.
Cynthia and I eat school lunch at separate tables.
She comes in one day with streaks of blue in her hair
a skirt that rides half way up her thigh bones.
Two years later she gets caught being truant
smoking cigarettes with three boys

over in a corner of the school yard.
On weekends I still see her out there
helping her father work on the cars.
Her overalls black as ink and her hair cropped
short as my brother's now.
I want to tell her that it doesn't suit her
but am afraid.

Cynthia was my friend.
When I was ten she gave me a valentine.
I still have its empty case in a box of childhood
treasure my parents store away for me.
She liked bologna sandwiches.
My favorite was salami with mustard and cheese.
We used to share our devil dogs
dream of summers on Long Island by the sea.
We grew away from each other.
She stopped waiting on the stoop to see when
I'd come out the front door.
I wanted to leave that place even back then.
Maybe she knew she would always stay.
In high school she won the Shop Mechanics Award.
I spent three years serving on the school literary magazine
but in truth nobody really knew me.
Since then no one has ever given me a valentine's box
like the one she did.
The red crushed velvet heart
all the paper cubbies inside like catacombs emptying.
One yellow plastic rose.

Yellow Yarn

Don't be gone long
my mother told me.
I had $1.45 in my palm
enough for a loaf of bread, caramel candy.
The store was four blocks over
by Reitmann's Bakery.
I was twelve years old
felt almost grown up.
My baby brother was jealous
because he had
to stay home.

The car that side walled me
never showed any lights.
It was beige, rusted
with its radio blasting.
Somebody put their coat over my legs.
It would be a long time
in the hospital.

It happens.
Being thrown off course.
I survived.
Grew quiet.
Buried myself in books
had casts up my legs.
Nobody but my family wrote on them.

Later the boys at school called me *a loser*
for always shying away.
I found another place to live in.
Pretended I could make the world
into yellow yarn
climb mountains
take the leg brace off that some sinister
tyrant had planted

fly over the fire escape
dilapidated houses
pigeon poop
see heaven
inside the grail
run the mile in four minutes
show God how compliant, resilient
devotional
the girl with a vanquished body
can be.

Ivy

Martha had red Dorothy shoes, many dresses.
Ivy couldn't compete with that.
Her mama wore no-nonsense clothes
worked long hours, had lost the sun in her bed.
Your clothes are drippy Martha told her.
I'm playing with Jorie. She has pierced ears
with pearl earrings and a purple slip on.

The next day Ivy told her mama
she wanted different clothes.
Pretty ones she said.
You're already pretty, sweetie, you don't need clothes to see that.
Ivy didn't feel better after her mother's words.
She poked through her closet
found the strappy sandals from last year that still fit
a butterfly clip she'd rescued from the playground
her soiled pink socks with lace trim.
She felt better now.

Next morning teacher did circle time as usual
then calendar, then talk about the day's projects.
They cut shreds of colored paper from magazines
to glue onto the piñata the class was making.
Finally it was snack time then play
in the little area outside the door.
Oh Martha, see what I brought today.
Martha had a purple dress on with pearly
buttons and patent leather shoes.
No, what? Not your stinky patched jeans?
No.
What then? Martha didn't have much patience.
Don't you see my hair? Look close.
Oh. An old butterfly clip. Where'd you get that?
I found it and it shines in the light.
There are sort of diamonds in it.
Martha was busy on the plastic slide

and barely looked.
Ivy continued *I've got my sandals on and pink socks
the color of Mrs. Slockum's peonies.*

Martha didn't hear.
She'd already walked away.
All knowing, six years old
she was off to find Jorie
who was wearing a glitter snowflake top
and fashionably short pastel skirt
never needed to please anyone
but herself.

The Ring

When Izzy decided to go to war with Katherine
it was over the stupidest thing—
the 25 cent jade ring with fake gold band
they'd swiped from the quarter machine
at Franklin's department store when, after a little jimmying
the jammed coin rewarded their gumption
with a plastic bubble prize.
It's mine claimed Izzy. *I turned the knob.*
Not true! I opened the slot and it dropped straight into my hand.
It's a mini miracle and you watch: it will fit perfectly on my middle finger.
She popped it out of its plastic bubble
pinched the adjustable back, slipped it on
and of course it was indeed a perfect fit.
That's not fair said Izzy, red in the face.
It's no miracle, you took it and made it fit your own finger.
But Katherine put on one of her superior smiles
and admired her hand.
You are so jealous, Izzy.
I go to church and Sunday school, that's how you get rewarded here.
Izzy just sped off on her bike anxious to work out a revenge.
Katherine was selfish and self-serving and loathsome
and so fake religious it made the cross puke.

Over the next week the real slingshots began.
Katherine's Maddie doll suddenly grew a smashed blue eye.
Izzy's bike lost its tire pump and the rubber horn was slit.
One day Katherine found her school locker
plastered with scorpion stickers.
Izzy's math notebook went missing
and a plastic skull turned up in her backyard.

Two months pass.
The ring with the fake jade stone gets lost
when Katherine's baby sister Emmie accidentally swallows it.
Katherine, who refuses to take this as an unlucky sign

claims it means that most likely one day
Emmie will inherit her gifts
walk on water with a surety nobody can resist.

Izzy asks her mother to remove Grandma Morin's
crucifixion picture from the living room wall
flings away her inherited blue rosary.
On the last Sunday before Easter
Katherine goes to mass, prays that Izzy will repent
or else stub her toe and break her arm climbing the big maple.
Izzy wants a lightning rod to frazzle the ends
of Katherine's blonde curls
as if finding God is a minefield of crunched barrettes
innocence bleeding.

Torched By Lightning

I knew it was dumb to be out under that tree
but somehow you just don't imagine
lightning will strike you.
My grandma says my heart could
have stopped forever
the way it knocked me to the
ground unconscious.
My brother just stood there
screamed for my mother.
She was down the road at Josie's house
looking in on the twins
who had croup, their two bodies
pale and thin as twigs.

Being struck by lightning when you're eight years old
does something to you
alters the brain chemistry maybe
makes it harder to see flies on the wall
welts on the trees
you like your chubby body better after
listen to the nuns with a rapt ear
thank the earth for saving you
helping you to come out of this
reformed and gaping.
The doctor at the hospital said
in seven out of ten cases like this
the person never gets up, walks away.

After that sparks scared me, fire crackers
the sound of pistols exploding
flashes of power failure
screen doors slamming
boys who crush lightning bugs in their hands.

Every sound of thunder
I donned rubber soled sneakers
closed all the windows
made mama tear every plug out of the socket.

Later, when I was camping one August
up Mount Monadnock with my first boyfriend
and the thunder started coming
flashes of lightning electrified the whole sky
I slid in the tent, zipped up every flap
broke into a cold sweat and nothing
not even the leaven of his kisses
his arms cupped tight around
could soothe me.

Already I knew death was a swinging door
can splinter childhood
gobble lifetimes
make you old before your time
place an axe where peonies used to be
force you to listen.

Sunday

When my mother wore her gold plated brooch
that bright insignia of the old country
up on the collar of her weary suit
she walked with a certain determination, vigor
that made her look younger than the sagging chin
rouged cheekbones that tried to conjure heaven as Sunday best.
I was nine, looked silly in my knee socks, buck shoes.
No child of mine will ever look like a Polish orphan she'd say.

In the Immaculate Conception Church on Grange Street
we always sat on the left side two thirds of the way back
where the pews were more shaded from the light
pouring in through the stained glass windows
and I imagine my mother hoped god wouldn't notice
our shabby things, no one would care that we'd only been
in this country a year and my father was not in attendance.
He was a self-proclaimed *heathen* but my mother still took pity
loved him with suet on the bread, perogies, kisses.
Six days a week she spent washing other people's clothes.

Dear Father in Heaven forgive us our sins she'd murmur
while fingering her blue crystal rosary.
People in front of us would turn their heads curious.
I'd look the other way
didn't understand why we needed forgiving
for coming to this country where nobody seemed to care
where my father worked in a tire factory ten hours a day
tried to pick up extra jobs come Saturdays when somebody
might blow a fuse, need extra sockets in the hallway.
I delivered newspapers.
My sister helped mama wash clothes, repair busted zippers
hems nobody had time to mend.

Were we sinners not living up to the mark?
My mama seemed to think so.
Scrubbed my mouth out with soap.

Said my complaints over too much potato, not enough meat
made for ingratitude in a scarce world.
Was I the greedy boy with too big an appetite
not enough friends?

I cheated a couple of times, never gave back the change
for the paper delivery payments
found a skateboard in the back alley with one wheel broken
took it home instead of waiting to see if some
other child would claim it.
My mama scolded me hard for that one.
Said it was outright stealing and I'd better
take it back this instant.
For days I watched the alley, the skateboard rotting in the rain.
Mama said God has no patience for sinners
who take other people's things
aren't satisfied with their own.
Jesus rewards the good who follow his commandments
the priest said in his sermon.
They are the chosen and shall not hunger and thirst in God's land.

I am waiting for God's promise
for my father to get his electrician's license
and my mother to have less callouses on her hands.
A roast or two once in a while
and a car that works well enough to take us
out of the city on Sundays for a drive.
They say the countryside here is a spill of poppies, crocus
cows grazing unperturbed over the hills
enough farms to feed the city
folks sell crates of fresh milk, cheese, apples by the road.
Then my father will lose his limp, start to dance again
my mother will slip open the hard knot that anchors her hair.

It is Sunday.
I am still waiting.

Easter

April, flushed with tulips
Good Friday fish
new patent leather shoes
to see Christ into heaven.

My mother calls from the bedroom
don't forget the dog
to feed him, she means.
I find it curious Christ could
multiply the modest manna
till the baskets are bottomless
and the apostles pass them out
with their astonished hands
while the rest of us keep sinking.

My mama has bought me a straw hat
mint colored dress that she says
slims the width of my waist.
I am practicing for my First Communion
when I get the white snap purse
the holy bible, blue crystal rosary.
The bible pages are edged in gold
and there are pictures in color
to remind me of heaven.

My brother says I dream a lot
am a chump for epistles, catechism class
look at our neighbor he says.
He's talking about Mr. Thadacus, Greek Orthodox
who's spent years attending the altar service on Hillside.
My brother says *Look at him now! He's got cancer
all through his body, only a few months to live.
He lost his only son in Iraq.*

So that's the reward he gets for keeping God all day in his head?
I'd rather take my chances on myself
have my eyes open.

That's my brother for you—the realist
he's always been like that
practical as evenly spaced nails
and just maybe he'll turn out to be
the savior of his own life.

Me. I'm of another stock—the sackcloth variety.
The fallen cushion.
The one who get scuffed up in every roll
of cardboard boxes down cut glass hills.
The girl who imagines fish jumping
through plate glass windows when there's no way out
Mr. Thadacus waking up to find the miracle
of an untreacherous angel by his bed.

I predict the sun will be brilliant on Easter Day.
My brother forecasts rain, tells me no one
will see my mint dress shrouded under the rain mac
that those patent leather shoes I keep so shiny
will be caked with mud, he even predicts dog shit
from someone's orphaned pet.

We ate hot cross buns from the bakery today
walked with mama up to the Grand Union
to get fish for the evening meal.
My dad, who works two jobs, goes to night college
will have scallops as a treat since he doesn't like fish.
On Sunday he will be coaxed to Easter mass
dress up like the rest of us.
I will avoid Sister Rosalind with her dark habit
who has no patience for messy little girls.

My father will remember the catholic orphanage
he was raised in, his no bicycle past.
We won't talk about any of this for another 20 years.

The sun will stream through the stained glass window.
The priest's mouth an empty hole
waiting for the inspiration of God's words to enter.
All of us will be there—
the lame Mrs. Lucy with her tiny body, sturdy cane
the Irish family with the four girls
a set of twins taking up the whole pew
Mr. Gilroy with his immaculate shoes
whose father owned the old meat shop
on 135th that was robbed last week
my mama in her spike heels and black rayon dress
reminding men of another kind of heaven.
All the erasures and allowances we must make
for the devote nature of our hands
to rise into bird prayer.

Lizzy's Meditation Garden

In April of her senior year, my cousin Lizzy
built herself what she called a meditation garden.
She's not going to let you play there.
That's all I heard.
We lived in the three-family house
two doors down with too many stray cats
always begging my mama for milk at the back door.
A rusted baby stroller, my busted two wheeler
and weeds grew in our yard.
Bamboo and poppies wouldn't even look good there.

I didn't know about private space
not having to share your big black and white
glazed cookie with your little brother
about sitting for half an hour cross-legged
burning incense
with a tray of fancy jasmine tea steaming.

We peeked through the fence. Alice and I.
Lizzy was my cousin, daughter of my
mother's oldest sister, Iris.
She had carrot red hair and too many freckles.
Said she agreed to babysit us only
to save money for Indian clothes and the
trip to find the great white elephant
she'd undertake someday.

Alice and I rolled our eyes.
We knew there were no elephants let alone
great white ones in Queens
thought Lizzy was better off getting
the new patent leather shoes in the window
of Mays Department Store or else saving
for one of those just slightly broken down
beach cottages you always see in Coney Island
with the For Rent sign dug into the dirt.

Imagine seagulls, pink beach tubes, white sand
a week's worth of cotton candy right outside your door.
Can we come in? Can we come in? we'd ask her.
Meditation is not for silly little girls.
So we'd jump rope instead, play marble games
bring out the tea set for my old Shirley Temple doll
with her dimpled smile, who was slowly losing her curls.
Secretly Alice and I plotted for the third Saturday in April
when I knew Iris was taking Lizzy on a shopping trip
into the city for that prom dress she needed
now that she agreed to go to her stupid high school prom
with Chuck DiAngelo whose father owned the pizzeria
up on Hillside that burnt down bad
in a mysterious fire three years ago.
Be careful your dress isn't flammable, we'd tease her.
She said she was going for nothing ordinary
and would talk her mother into a silk sari from India
with jazzy thongs to match.
Fat chance—we thought to ourselves.
Iris Mackey was just like my mama
born of the same family of practical, no nonsense
shoe dwellers, crisp kitchen aprons, polyester dresses
that don't propagate wrinkles and always have give.

It was on the third Saturday in April that Alice and I used
a coat hanger to get the latch open on the backyard gate.
I knew from my mom that Lizzy's dad was out at the shop
doing overtime repairs on some Volvo a guy brought in.
Inside the gate we marveled at the mats, the big
Indian print cloth she'd tacked to the wall of the garage
the plump colorful cushions, some with sewn mirrors
that nestled against the wall. There were candle holders
an incense ring, dried flowers wound into small bouquets
on a plastic crate covered with cloth to make a side table.
Two pots of orange poppies sat on either side.
On one hand, I thought it was totally impractical

the rain would sop right through the trellis work
the cushions, rattan mats.
On the other hand, I found it beautiful, like another world
a special place away from the thump of stick bats and kick ball
the stench of cars, gas lawnmowers
Mrs. Riley's noisy hedge clippers
the too many empty beer cans ditched in the alley
come Friday nights when the older kids had nothing to do.
I wanted to stay there, ring the brass bell
have my tea delivered along with big
black and white iced cookies from Reitmann's Bakery
and not have to share a bit of them with anyone else.
Alice said, *Come on. We've seen it now. Let's get out of here.*

A week went by. Lizzy didn't get her Indian sari or thongs
for the high school prom. Mama told me Aunt Iris insisted
on a practical empire waist long dress they found
on the markdown rack at Bloomingdales.
Said it was lavender and could easily be taken up to regular
street length once the prom was over.
Mama asked me if Alice or I had gone snooping
in Lizzy's little garden.
I said, *No, mama.*
But I guess Lizzy knew that somebody had visited there
claimed the incense burner, bouquets of flowers
had all been rearranged—and now it's no good to her.
Mama told me she claims it will never be the same
now that the privacy's left it.

A week after that it was all taken down.
One afternoon Alice and I peered through the fence.
The woven mats—gone. Gone—the Indian print tacked
to the garage wall, gone the incense burner, the antelope
candle holders, gone the Buddha
the yellow embroidered cushions
the two pots of poppies red as heaven.

All swept away.
Only a concrete path, a garage and a side shed
left where Lizzy Mackey's meditation garden had once been.

She looked stiff on her prom night.
I came out to see.
Mama was taking pictures of Lizzy on the porch.
The dress was a starched cotton
that would never go limp or swirly
with a pearl buttoned high neck and overly gathered sleeves.
But the lavender color was pretty.
My Aunt Iris had pinned Lizzy's long hair
up in a french kind of knot
and then teased the top hair a bunch to get it to lift.
I hardly recognized her with her thick black mascara, cherry lips.
Chuck pinned a corsage on her dress—not red as the
fire of Lizzy's once oriental poppies but pink
durable carnations with sprigs of baby breath
that stay in place where you pin them and don't
stand out like a high heel roller coaster in the wind.
I felt bad after that.
Wished Alice and I had never snuck into Lizzy's back garden
that third Saturday in April.
Not a soul ever learned about it.
In November when I asked mama if Lizzy was still wanting
a rayon scarf from Nepal, silver ring this Christmas
she laughed, said *No, darling, she's saving for community college
her car license, has come to her senses.*

PART FOUR
Midnight Plagues

Jonah Swallowed Up By The Whale

When Jonah was swallowed by the whale
nothing came back out again.
Maybe my father told me that
because he wanted me to listen
stop apostrophing the moon
making my life into a handrail
so steep God couldn't climb it
with his glass legs.

I was ten.
Never fit gracefully into the Easter coat
two sizes too small
my mother bought for me.
It was meant for another girl
one with perfect teeth, no hips
starched white blouse collars.

Five years later my father suffered a stroke.
His voice stammered after that
and when he spoke of Jonah and the whale
it came out as broken syllables.
My mother got her job back selling clothes
in the junior section of Gertz Department Store
and a state nurse came two afternoons a week
to check on my dad.

He never apostrophed the moon
and look what happened to him.
Now my father stumbles over words
warns *The world has surprises, be ready for them.*
Can't count on anything to save you.
As if God has been erased from his head

like a shoeless man who can't find
the way home.

I anchor safety pins to my bed.
Straight pin the torn hems
I'll get around to mending one day
latch the windows at every lightning storm
let none of my lunch meat migrate
from the grip of the bread.

This is what loss can do to you—
my mother with her black fishnet stockings
accentuating the curve of her legs
the men eyeing her as she sashays up the aisle
to the third row of the church pews
my brother baiting cops with the size
of his truck wheels, holed up in his black painted
room all night not talking to anybody
me—dining on angel cake in giant spoonfuls
out of our red glass bowl
trying to tell myself that Jonah never got swallowed
by the whale, and my father will walk again
and my mother doesn't care a dime for those guys
driving by our front door
that God likes brokenness
girls who devour the world's sins
drown them in cake batter
better than the rest.

Cellophane

It was pestilence that saved her
15 years old with long streaked hair
angel food white and succulent
the steps he led her into his bed
those older hands
those terribly worn hands with
the calluses of smashed days towing.

She cut his words out
his tongue, his eyes grey curtain
his face that held nothing but brute wind
a body hard as steel pressing down
scissored all of it away
the way her mother had scissored herself
out of the family photograph albums
the way her brother cuts up paper
scalps it till it bleeds in a puddle
of useless ends on the floor.

Silence. It was the silence that would save her.
She knew about that, courted it
wrapped herself in its cellophane folds
till the world didn't turn blue anymore.

There are words that never find flight
fancy that gets buried here
people who must erase themselves to live
stamp out the man with his chain lit cigarette burning
stamp out the host they once laid on your tongue
vanished now
in the bowls of white cake batter
the lumps creamed with a wooden spoon
the bounty of it
the secrets it never betrays
when your lips press toward oblivion

each mouthful a silent corridor
that nuptials the torn allegiances
of your heart.

She let him trample her body
but he could never despoil her words.
They went inwards.
She learned how to hold up the sky
screw herself into skimpy rayon dresses
let you see how a being can be
vandalized
again and again and again
and still live to tell about it
in some stammer of song.

Crows

There were crowbars on his tongue
wax with a high polish.
He opened my drawers once
just once
let the crème camisoles
white panties fall derelict
onto the floor.

I was fifteen.
Fifteen.
He was too old for me
chalk walled my garden without regret
lent his surgical words
to the moon's apostolic longing.

I cuffed my ears
wanted to feign oblivion
watch seagulls fly.
He wore sleek clothes the color of midnight.
Tore the pearl buttons off my blouse.
Shook me till I was raw, speechless
where words cave into a dark hole.

I tried to say -
I have the moon in my chest
a chorus of waxwings
what you trespass now
will come back to you later
black as crows.

He didn't know how to listen.
All his days now seeded in dark shoes
crows nesting.

Black Rayon

Christy's mother said
bad girls always die of their past
as if it's best to keep my body
tucked in white panties
to bypass the rain.

I was eight. Slept in baby dolls
ate cake batter when the moon
couldn't find me
attended catechism class
imagined if I prayed right
God would raise me up with my
thorn wreathed heart burning.

Never suspected there'd be crowbars
a father who busts out doors
a mother hot as sin in a July heat wave
baiting the guy in the Buick
till one day he's found folded over
with two front teeth missing.

My mother wore a black rayon cocktail dress
the day she married my father.
I've seen the pictures—it was curvy and strapless
and Christy's mother would say loaded with sin.

Who can speak for a busted life
my mother sashaying across the pocket lawn
in that skimpy kimono
painting our parlor walls black late night
with cigarette after cigarette burning

the way later she will splatter across the floor
with her morning tea cup
never get back up.

I remember eating angel food cupcakes
cake batter, cookies, like there was no tomorrow.
Drowning the day in good pinafores
smiles that leak nothing of betrayal
remember my mother's gold ring
that shined some kind of endurance
even in the open casket
after her heart splintered
and she fled from this world.
I remember the stoic priest, funeral offering
Christy's low cut red dresses that in high school
courted sin the confessional box tried to erase
the way I cling to marriage
like a prayer book, a benevolent father
who never devours what he eats.

Midnight.
You screw the bulb of dancing lights into the socket
look for my sheerest panties.
Want a tiger inside your bed
woman whose hope never scratched the walls
witnessed a life gone to ruin.

Pleasures

When Jessica told her folks
she wouldn't stay at school full day
the foundation of their house lifted.
Her father was Portuguese, worked at the tannery
never wanted to imagine a daughter of his
staying home with the dishes, later on busing tables
pregnant with two kids.

Jessica was seventeen back then.
Never fit in.
Her clothes were always too small for her.
The boys called her *Titanic* and she hated it.
Her lunch bag loaded with corn chips
a boiled egg, those vanilla custards
her mom baked that all of us bribed
with devil dogs to get a scoop.

In May we didn't see her anymore.
Mrs. Jacobs erased her name
from the week eleven science report list.
Her locker was stripped of its masking tape
and the new boy from California snagged it.
I thought she changed her father's mind after all.
Imagined her in a print smock helping her mother
pin out laundry and then hanging off the fire escape
spending the afternoon reading novels
while the rest of us slaved in overcrowded rooms
rote memorized civil war names.
My mom said not to talk about it
that Jessica was off at her aunt's house in New Jersey
and who knows when she'd come back.

We never heard the word *Titanic*
ringing through the halls after that.
Vanilla custards disappeared
along with her soupy stories, unruly black hair.

That summer I bicycled up and down the hills of the city
giving arts and crafts projects to kids in the parks.
My brother got in trouble with the law
for hurling obscenities at a policeman
who stopped his truck
and my mama seemed to be off in the distance
dreaming of a different life
eating bowls of fudge marble ice cream
late night in her web chair.

Come September Jessica came back.
She looked bigger. Didn't talk to anyone.
Was seen moping round the yard bagging dead leaves.
Called me one Saturday to go window shopping
over at the Mays Department Store in Jamaica
but warned me she had nothing to spend.
By now I was working part-time at the retail shop
that employed my mom, who'd overwhelm me
with the size nine dresses she'd put aside
anxious to see if my body would squeeze into them.
I had to work, didn't see Jessica that day.
A week later it was my dad who heard the sirens blasting.
Says he nearly cut his throat in the middle of his shave.
Jessica's mom was wheeled into the ambulance
never came home again.
Heart attack my mom told me.

Jessica didn't call me again.
She had three brothers and a dog tired dad.
The tannery was on hard times and I saw him
working the Quick Mart on Hillside one Sunday
when I slide in for a box of devil dogs
I didn't want anybody to see.

Come November Jessica and I ran into each other.
Both of us big and gawky and not really fitting in.

I knew we had a lot in common
but never managed to own up to it.
How you doing, I said.
*"O.K. Lost a baby last summer from some guy
my brother Denis met at the speedway.
My dad was glad though. With my mom gone it sure would have
complicated things. What are you up to?*
Jessica said all this so matter of fact
I didn't know what to reply—
*Sorry about your mom, Jessica.
I'm stressed over college applications
doing two jobs after school
to save money for next year.*
I never told her or admitted to myself that
I was gone all the time because it was too hard
to be there at our house watching my dad
angry, jobless, tearing open rejection letters
sulking behind the newspaper headlines at the
dining room table everyday
and that I didn't recognize my mother anymore.
*I'm making a vanilla custard tomorrow.
The boys are home and dad's not working.
Remember how you used to trade off your cupcakes
and devil dogs at school for just a taste of it.
Want me to bring you over a bowl? I make it
same as my mama did—follow her recipe to the T
except for the shaved nutmeg on the top—
that's my own creation.*

*Thanks but I'm on a diet again. My mom says
I need to lose twenty pounds before
any boy will even look at me.*

*Maybe you should have a bowl of vanilla
pudding anyway. Just for the pleasure of it.
There aren't that many pleasures left in this world.*

I heard the sad tinge in her voice.
We laughed.
*O.K. Come by at five. I'll show you my class ring
and the cool snow globe and new album I got for Christmas.*

We were a skewered odd pair—
eating our bowls of vanilla pudding
out on the back porch where my mama couldn't see us
and dad wouldn't be hammering and chain sawing
because it was Sunday and he said everybody
was decreed a day of rest in this world.
Jessica and I lulled in the vanilla pudding.
Rolled our mouths in the folds of it.
Let the pudding slide down our throats
exquisite
one pure heavenly spoonful at a time.

Devotion

The palm reader didn't give my mama
such good news—she said my fourteen year old road
looked hard as nails with too many leavings
an armload of rain.
But I saw the way she snatched our money
gave a reading that was not one minute past
the half hour mark we'd paid for
and decided she was a hoax.

My mama cried when we came back outside
said I had no idea how many nights
she'd stayed up sleepless worrying for me
the shyness, too much time alone
heart murmur and all.

I think it is my destiny to be a star I consoled her.
We were back in the small kitchen
dishing out coffee cake, which is what
she and I always did when we wanted to feel better
wanted to forget the clothesline
silly palm reader with her red-dyed hair
bill collector tacking his notice slip on the door.
What makes you say that? she queries
as if she needs proof, something sure to vouchsafe
that my life won't turn out disastrous.
I feel it in my bones.
Like God is drumming up a plan for me
I just need to stay slow and listen.

When God comes, she says
I'll ask for two new porch steps to replace the rotted ones
a garden that grows decent peonies
and a red party dress with my body gone slim....
a man who knows how to take zippers up and down, sing.

He must be tender too
no lying
and dependable.

My mama licked the crumbs from her fork.
Said we better have another piece of cake
ready ourselves
with our cups of tea, our honey
devotion.

PART FIVE
The Visitation

The Climb

When Madame LaRosa stepped onto the ladder
she'd placed to reach the camellias
the children were fretful
not for her good intentions
but for the unstable way the ladder's metal legs
tottered in the sun streaked dirt
the chiffoned weight of her
as she climbed each step for the promise of coral
camellias with their yellow tongues drizzling
and the fall they anticipated any moment
when the ladder tilted, gave way
and Madame LaRosa found herself
not feather light, weightless
but instead mired in dirt.

But Madame LaRosa
beneath her wisps of cotton and chiffon
had surer feet than the children's imaginings
reached the highest boughs beside the porch eave
unpinned the black clippers from her skirt
cut vigorously till the season of boughs pierced with coral
spread across the wide swath of her arms.
Then slowly, one step at a time, descended the ladder
and brought them down to her children.

Yes. She was wise and weighted.
To the children now, Madame LaRosa
with her floating chiffon, wild loop of hair
could do just about anything
even fly.

Taken

Christopher said I was a caged lover
who always fled from his bed.
It was true but I didn't want to admit it.
It was his bed, his life, his terms
and I couldn't see my face in them.
Ran as far as my legs would carry me
till a day or two later
the phone rang
sweet words
sweet lips
forgiveness soft as angora
and before you know it we were
rolling on top of each other again
and then I wanted to go home.

It was no surprise to anybody but me
when we broke up that August
after he finished school.
All July he'd followed me everywhere
had his duffle bags moved into my space.
Told me I'd fry my skin if I kept sun tanning.
He was my handsome Chicano, didn't fry his skin.
I was eight years older than him and maybe
he was already conscious of the lines that might
start forming at the corners of my eyes.
When he left I had my tiny apartment back
my bike rides by the river
the big alone I was used to
but I felt like a sledge hammer
had crushed me beside the wall.
Couldn't imagine I'd stand back up again.
Couldn't eat for days except popcorn
out on the fire escape at midnight.
Told everyone I'd probably never write
another poem but simply sink in water

and the authorities would have to scoop me
out with a fish hook.
Nothing left for that other lover
you
with your thousand needs pawing.
But I did rise.
Life rises.

Gulls

Yes he was younger
I admit that.
By eight years.
Not jaded yet.
No comfortable suits, four wheel drives
business card towing.

Yes we made love together.
Yes it was like another world
someone had kept for me.
So much gentleness.
I couldn't believe the talc of his hands
as if tenderness was an open stair
invitation from heaven.

I was 37 and Anglo.
He was 29, Chicano, and delicate.
His words blew soft gulls
into my bed.

I started to believe in God again
the curved loveliness of the swan
magnificence of the wheat field.

Later we would not be able to talk
across the space of a cafe table
or long distance phone line
as if it was too fragile
too extinguishable
this rare pearl
we clutched tight so long ago
in our bed.

Clemency

Lover, that's what he called her
as if she were sultry, appealing
and not just 48 and worn down
with two small kids
a pocket watch in her head.

She tried to imagine it different.
Maybe 20 pounds thinner
toned down legs.
Her bikini panties an ample version
of paradise calling.
How she would take him there
again and again and again
till he wouldn't live to tell about it.
Struck dead by the over stimulation.

It would be clemency then.
Of a sort.
Red embalmed, scent of hubris
old shoes, musty closet
the curved arms of the wire rim glasses
still matted to his hair.

What does it feel to die in ecstasy
like this
so erect nothing can fail you
to finally drive some banana yellow
convertible
like a bombshell
with nobody home?

Remembering

You imagine that you never loved him
he never set foot in this door
dug in steer manure
countless wheelbarrows of compost
crushed egg shells
tilled the first veg bed that ushered in summer—
squash vines, Roma tomatoes, bush beans
overtaking the yard thistle.

What if he had been scarred
fire burned, short as a toad
slant as a board with too much buckle
would you still have loved him?
What if the old disused sauna hut
was relieved of its porcelain sinks
resurrected with a new stove
would you have lounged naked
his voice lending you hours of discourse
those erudite proclamations that stall the sea
would your bodies still have twined
into the sky's lumbering
road the river of merciful stars
that lead out past skunk cabbage
into the fields of clover
where Neruda's odes swoon
on supine knees?

Has it really been twelve years
of dissolution and emerald shoes
sanctity strung out on diminutive
clotheslines, the colored lights
of the window's breaking?

It is February.
Some would say you are not young anymore
have two small children paddling in and out

the back door.
Who would have thought you could
forge a life like this one
piercing the skin of loneliness
and walking through to the other side?
How could you have known
six years ago that when you ran out of that farmhouse
loaded the truck with your three-year-old boy child
that you'd still hold those invisible threads
that trump sensible socks, practical seasons
come back to grow this hodgepodge garden
amaryllis blooms big as Christmas
thistle stabbing the rosemary by the door
the blue yard swing
all this preamble
these nubby pathways
this song.

With Child

Tetrahedron.
Isosceles triangle.
He knew all of that but she didn't
didn't know how to fix the yard's leaking hose
the downspouts that keep breeding ponds
around the foot of the steps.
Not that she apologized, mind you.
The mind can only hold so much rubble
in it before it busts.
She knew that.
After five months at that place
they said she'd have to keep taking stock
of her life, *be vigilant*
keep the stress level turned down
her feet planted firmly against somebody's
ivy strewn wall.

Her socks didn't match.
She could fry eggs, make dandelion soup
take him on walks come midnight
when the streetlamps dim
the snake of alleys lead down to the
sea's moonlight hissing.

He knocked over her German Hummel child
the day he entered her house
never noticed the thirsty spider plants
dog's food bowl
planted two piles of detective books
alongside the bed
ignored her blue rosary, rabbit slippers.

She wanted to tell him about heaven
the fluorescent bugs that litter her hair
movable toadstools

but he was 38 and sensible
with a day job, stock options
automatic bill paying.

November came with its expired leaves
icy heart
froze the water pump
dug big holes in the gravel
till her tires seemed to lift then dip.
She nailed Christmas lights up above the porch
brought out her carol book, bread maker.

A storm hit December 16th
knocked out the power
buried the farmhouse in three feet of snow.
They reloaded the old parlor stove every two hours
lit candles, kerosene lamps, melted snow
in cast iron pots on the wood burning cooker.
He knew so many ways to say a word
and almost mean it
like *forever* and *baby* and *tired old soul*
and *abortion*.

And then it would be spring
and the migrant workers hands would already be
suckling the strawberry fields
and their daughters would come with their happy bellies
faith in the Virgin
arrive with her at the low-income midwife clinic in Hillsboro.
And she'd been told to keep her feet planted.
Now she was pregnant.
Her feet, anchored beside the ivy strewn wall
began to rise.

The Recovery

When William came down to the virgin's side
he found her asleep beyond waking
so we're told he stayed there--
sweet vigil--till the first cock's crow
till the sun bestowed its benevolent face
upon the room's reckless.

She was eighteen, the youngest daughter.
Perhaps no man had ever traced
his body beside her.
Warm body pressed in sack cloth
pressed in sheet folds.
Her scarcity bred of waiting
on winter's wanton
the blue deathbed upon her lips.
The first trespasses always the hardest
to be coaxed from your bed.

Sister Teresa called her *the chosen one*
because of her hair's abundance
guileless genuflections
cakes bred more of angel than thorns
claimed this girl could marry spring rain
float in taciturn air, make repair.

William smudged his finger across his forehead.
Sweet vigil.
The room heavy shuttered, sick basined
the washcloths wrung out to dry
dovecots absent of morning fire
a young girl's reprise gone soft gloved.

Later, no one faltered her
for the wind's transgressions
scissor cropped her hair

in a blunt cut
nor tore away the amulets of love
that had entered her bed.

They say he was a good father
when the child came
visited at midnight
crept out before the sun's return.
Suckled him on meadow wort
lamb's clove, wolfs bane
drove in no hard stake.

By day, the girl bathed the child in
crystal waters, hyacinth, forest
dabbed him in resin, death
so he might learn how to worship
her hands a reprieve woven of the
devotional seeds of that bed.

No one outside the room witnessed
the miracle when it came.
All we know is that she rose up
her crushed petals reborn about the bed
Sweet William always vanished by dawn
before any words betray.

PART SIX
Conjuring it New Again

The Crank Box

It was a crank box
like my uncle Amele used to have
mohair and metal and a clap trap door
that could take your finger off
if it misbehaved.

Mama said to stay away
a grown up game
game where some get buried
in an avalanche of coin
others live in regret.

Bald Ridge was a strange place to play
God forsaken windswept corridor
tumbleweed barely nailed to the dirt.
All the men gathered there
traded wristwatches, cows, farm labor, manure
women's favors before the coins ran out.

That was the summer the well dried up
my father remortgaged the house
came and went
sent my brother to town once a week
for a bottle of whiskey he felt he'd earned.
We sat silent on the porch, listened
to the barnyard gate creak
smoothed stray stitches in the rag rug.
Mama swore my father loved that crank box
more than us
pressed its metal sides to his lips
as if it was heaven.
One night went off to Bald Ridge
never came back.

Mama claims it was the jangle
the lure of gold coins that raked him.

But I prefer a different story
that there was a man
buried in cow shit
deep up to his thigh bones
and no way to get out
and my papa, being a decent sort
who never gave a damn about hoarding money
strong as a bull raised on vetch and timothy
took the man, spread him out over his shoulders
and carried him up to the top ridge
where the moon meets the sun's downfall
and the sky turns mustard blue to amber again
and because we were a poor house
a house flanked with proper church going women
he knew there was no place there
for the stranger nailed upon his back
so he walked on
half sorrowful of what would be left behind
half resolute of the burden that had been
entrusted to him.

If there were gold coins
they were the hard of his faith
luster of his eyes burning.

Festival Of The Fishes

When Maria Torino came to our house
for the Festival of the Fishes
my mama was not ready
no braided garlic above the door
our shrine to the Virgin Mother
still cribbed with dead hollyhocks
the plastic Mickey Mouse toy my brother
had stashed there.
Maria, no, you cannot come in yet.
I am not ready for you.
All afternoon Maria Torino
had held the gilded cross
wrapped with blue rosaries in her left hand
in the other swung incense
from the brass ball of a long chain.
She was old now—75, maybe 80
every Festival of the Fishes she went up and down
the hills of the village, anointing the houses
believed it was her mission.

Papa had gone to work when a tourist
from the city broke down on the Guerro Road
and he earned $50 for repairing the fan belt
and giving the guy a tow.
Mama was ashamed of his hands
the grease embedded in them
and how the white shirt she'd washed special
seemed ruined because of his hands.

Maria Torino did not take no for an answer
not about the new stone wall for the cemetery
the help she needed to harvest her bean field
or the fact the Mayor himself must lead the festival parade
with the float of the Virgin Mary Shrine out in front
for the day to be right
for the holy one to bless this village

with another year of many fishes.
Maria Torino sat down at the table
by our window, shook her head
and began braiding the garlics
she saw in a basket by the cook stove.
In no time three long braids
were pegged to our front door.
My mama was crying, afraid she had let everybody down.
No matter, Rosa—you have been sick with the boy.
And Maria Torino stood up
relit her incense in the brass ball
cleared away the Mickey Mouse figure
and blessed our shrine to the Virgin Mother
dead hollyhock and all.
Bless this house and all who are in it.
Keep them out of harm's way, Virgin Mother
and with this she kissed each of our foreheads
offered us up one by one her crucifix with the blue rosary
then disappeared up the cobbled street
to the neighbor's door.

My mama said my papa had disgraced us with his dirty hands
and my brother's toys should never be allowed to migrate
onto the shrine table.
Then she slipped the apron back over her flowery dress
began rolling the flat breads
with Papa sneaking up on her now and then
planting a kiss along the back crease of her neck
while she fussed, half turned her shoulder away.

I was already sure mama had forgiven him
was making the flat breads just the way he liked
stuffed with dates, apricots, powdered sugar
so he could rest his weary feet in the old arm chair

delight in nibbling them
that after the parade was finished
and Mama had forgotten his dirty nails
she'd lead him back to their tiny bedroom
beyond the door.

Irene

Irene never told me her father died when she was eight
that her mom liked bourbon so well
she couldn't get up some mornings
and what we passed off as a disinclination for school
was really a hangover and too many bills.

I knew Irene for eleven years before our paths slit sideways.
Knew her from the seven year old thin as a tire spoke
with thick glasses through senior year when her hair
turned peroxide yellow and she put on too many pounds.
As far back as I remember people made fun of her.
First *poke weed* then *pug girl* then *where'd you get
those Magoo glasses* to *fat pig*
and *she's like a sausage strangled in a jacket*.

Nobody thought she was smart or boyfriend material.
Mrs. Strickland, the fourth grade teacher, picked on her
for being late, having too many unexcused absences.
She visited Mrs. Cauley, Irene's mother once
out at the trailer park off Reese Lane
said the place stank to high heaven
from too much renegade garbage
wilted geraniums, lazy hands.
I know all this because my mom was assistant
to the school nurse back then, always heard the gossip.

My sister Cass and I had to wear starched white blouses
checkered pinafores to school.
Nobody could complain about our lunch boxes
they were identical, disgusting vinyl with white cats
stamped all over them.
I tried to hide my Dalmatian napkin
toothpicked ham sandwiches
ate only the ham and threw away the bread
sat across from Irene, her 25 cent bags of nacho chips
frazzled hair.

We did have a few things in common like devil food dogs
dark chocolate cake outside that hid a creamy white center
we both loved them and I begged my mother to put in extra
so I could trade.

From early on I was chubby, over time Irene would catch up.
Both of us got pelted with rock infested snowballs
when the boys at recess were looking for easy targets.
Irene fought back.
I caved in crying or else ran to the principal's office and told.
After a while I became *teacher's pet* and Irene was *troublemaker*
and *dumb stick* which later became *dumb blonde*.

I tell you about all this not because I want you to take pity
on the way life treats people
or reproach me for not working harder
to get across some bridge that divided us
but because some things don't sit well in this world
don't right themselves like you always imagined they would
the pumpkin turned coach, rose petals, ball gown, celebrity.
You want to imagine Irene as yearbook editor
the slimmed down prom queen
I get to go to Vassar or NYU or Stanford
beguile everybody with the intellectual edge of my charms
not to the state school chalking up student debt
working three summer jobs
Irene not stuck forever at the Woolworth's counter
with the balloons a child can pop for a free ice cream
or marrying that jerk she ran off with to Kansas
the one who buried her in three kids
before fleeing to Chicago with a skinnier blonde.
Mom says she's back at the trailer park
works nights restocking shelves at the supermarket.
I'm at the state university studying English

still eating too many devil dogs
avoiding starched blouses, foil toothpicked
ham sandwiches wherever I find them.

Irene and I never became close friends.
Not really.
But maybe we knew each other
better than the rest.
She didn't have a library card
but she liked books—Dostoevsky, Kafka, Camus
in that class she was the one with the raised hand.
In high school she wanted to join the literary club
but nobody thought she was dependable enough
to make all the meetings.
The truth is she could be sitting in this dorm room at
this school studying for finals, munching too many chips
thinking about the AIDS epidemic
and I could be back there at Woolworth's
squirting ketchup and mustard on hamburger buns
pricking a balloon for the small blue boy
at the counter who hopes for a strawberry sundae.
I want you to know that it's not because
I was better or cleverer
or even more decent in the true sense of the word
but because things get dealt this way
and the world isn't fair.

But I try to tell myself
as consolation maybe, or is it remorse
that even from a clipped windowsill
it is still possible, in a certain hour
certain angle of unburdened refrain
for a woman stocking shelves at Frank's IGA
to truly witness the azalea rising up

the sheen of the afternoon light on her yard table
the way trees pocket our discontents
give their bodies over to the earth, the sky, the seasons
without claiming status
rise up equal for you and for me.

In My Story

Franz Jacobs may never recover himself.
Never find the lost leg or the lost wife
who left him three years ago when the
workman's comp checks ran out.
My father, solitary, writing job applications
at the kitchen table, says Franz
will go down the tubes at the rate he's going
but I have more faith than that
imagine him one day at Gerhards Bakery
down on Queens Boulevard
fingering the rye bread, raisin buns
when another hand inadvertently enters.
She'll be shy, taken back by the intimacy
of two strangers' hands, be wearing
the inconspicuous of a grey sweater
have already known what it's like to beg
for water, work a dead end job
nurse your brother dying of cancer
till there is nothing left of him, just bony
prayer books that doormat the wind.

He'll make a new start of it then.
First slow. A coffee and bagel.
He'll leave off the onions and lox.
Then later a movie down on 135th
hot pastrami sandwiches, a Yankee ball game.
He won't notice the runs up her stockings
the red eyes she has pyred to heaven
the shy way she keeps tearing herself away
from the nest of his arms.

Come Easter she arrives with a cherry pie
afterwards begins visiting a lot.
In June they set two web chairs out on the lawn
begin sitting the evenings away
waiting for the moon to enter.

My father stops yapping about handouts
and dead end lives, quits noticing Franz's garbage
since there are barely any beer cans anymore.
When the house gets painted in July
everybody's eyebrows raise.
Flamingo pink just the way she wants it
with dark green shutters that, she says
bring the aspect of trees to your door.
My dad goes over and helps with the trim work.
Afterwards we spread out glasses of lemonade.
My brother gobbles too many vanilla wafers
and I admire the color of her hair—
gone yellow as a summer wheat field.

In my story Franz
gets retrained in ventilator systems
eventually gets union pay.
His new princess doesn't die of heart disease
starts planting borders of crocus beside the front door
talks Franz into getting fitted with a new prosthetic.
After months of practice he wields it almost like
a brand new leg under his work pants.

My father forgets his past, the catholic orphanage
too many schools, one pair of shoes
wrestles with truculent angels
finally grows new wings
remembers the firm grip of our neighbor's hand
remembers my mother's waist
the curve of her thigh's making
her auburn hair turned golden blossoms
in the sun.

The Lesson

Heir Gotmann up on the third floor
in the midst of his 30 days of Lenten fast
may get too thin, die
or else beg for mercy -
cheesecake, his wife's strudel
good bagels by the bed
may gather his collection of Hummel figures
roll them in the starched tablecloth
forget his stout nagging wife
and fly out the window someday.

There must be many ways to enter heaven.
Death being one anchoress that can take us there.
Imagine the headlines -
Heir Gotmann, assistant auditor of Trumble & Blake
husband, father and clockmaker extraordinaire
found splattered across the pavement Friday
when the delirium of his Lenten fast failed him
and he leapt from his parlor window
mired in temporary despair.

or

Heir Gotmann, ex-assistant auditor of Trumble & Blake
snow globe repair person extraordinaire
disappeared suddenly Friday.
His wife said she glanced in the living room
in the midst of making her usual flat sided noodles
only to find his body lifting off the floor
and finally out the window.
It could be noted he was on his 30th day of a
Lenten fast and his wife confessed
with a certain amount of hesitation
that all propriety had left him
and he leapt from the parlor window

determined he could fly.
Disappeared floating outside the building
with only his boxer shorts on
a pair of red mittens, transistor radio.

I've become convinced there are myriad ways
to enter heaven
and death holds any number of surfaces
shapes and sizes
like the shoes we wear
the houses we live in
the sunless sky's wanton
the past that begs to come clean in our hands.

The Blue Ices

My friend Rosemary once told me
that all women dream of a small waist
the efficient conquest of body fat
a muscular life.
I quietly suspect
but did not try to convince her
that endless running
might turn out to be
injurious to the soul, to something soft
something delicate
we all hope will endure.

She thinks my problem is willpower
or lack of it
a diffidence to authority
to any circumstances the day wields
that taking control is an act of self-respect
and powerful women do not impulsively
eat food
wait by side windows
nibble the eraser off their blue pens.

I have never told her
the holy grail invents its face in me
that other people's pain might trump
our happiness when we pause
to consider the weight of it
and sometimes maybe nothing
makes sense in this world
at least not the way we've arranged it.
My body holds its indecency like
a secret hedge, a scroll only certain people
are ever meant to write on.
I like best lounging in overgrown grass
beside forgotten wide mouthed rivers.
My tongue is blue

from the blue ices I've sucked since childhood
rocket shaped missiles on a stick
from the ice chest
in the bite sized deli in Queens.
These blue ices always make the world
turn more decent
less cruel
almost noble
as I place their cool, sweet, compliant bodies
on my tongue and suck.

Mary Donahue

Mary Donahue prided herself
on her pies—huckleberry, rhubarb
with a hint of apple, crème custard
with chocolate grated on for a pretty face.

Like all decent girls we devoured
them tenderly.
No one can say we were shy of a
good whistle coming down the street
or afraid to nail ribbons to our hair
welcome pink onto the firmament
of our dress hems.
So it was with much surprise
the day Mary Donahue left us.
An ordinary day, not fitful in any way.

She came to choir practice the night before.
Was due at the milliner's shop bright
and early the next morning for her
coronation headdress to get sewn.
Mary Donahue—Spring Pageant Queen.
Each of us was a bit envious of her.
All that pie baking, and good teeth
and not an ounce of malice.
Trask Phillips had already noticed her
kept leaving anonymous daffodils
beside her school locker.
We all knew they were from him.
His left leg had a slight limp
and one boot made thicker than the other.
Said it happened at birth and he had
nothing to do but make the best of what was left .
There was a lot left -
that shock of blonde hair, a smile
that could melt any girl and smart as a whip
at least that's what Fanny's mom says.

She helps at the school and told us
he had the best college entry scores
of anybody she'd tallied
that Mrs. Willis, the high school teacher
was checking on big scholarships for him.

Mary Donahue knew she'd be in Prineville forever.
Even the fortune teller up in Madras told her so.
Said she had long life lines, lots of rootedness.
As for me—that I'd break men's hearts, move a lot.
We went out for vanilla floats after that.
Mary said she wished we could trade fortunes
and I thought she was crazy back then.
She lived in the white farmhouse with the big
front porch and a yard littered with kittens
knew how to cook, milk goats in 4-H Club
make cheese, set her heart on any man and
they'd probably melt for her.
I was already a mess.
Not one boy looked at me except to call
piggy. Neither svelte or culinary
I lived in the three family house in town
across from the Sears Roebuck
and every morning my mama swore it was
all the cars in the parking lot that sooted up
the windows so we could barely see.
She was always wielding a dust cloth
ammonia, dreams of the beach.

Mary Donahue never left a note
a word, nothing that any of us heard.
Never made it to the milliner's shop, Miss Casey's
that Wednesday first thing.
After a few days the sheriff's office ruled out foul play
because her big suitcase and clothes were missing.

It was peculiar how Trask Philip's limp got worse.
He started to stutter and the scholarships
Mrs. Willis was working on mysteriously dried up
while we waited on news of Mary D.

Two years later I was going to college over on the
other side of the mountains in the Willamette Valley
when I saw a girl sipping a shake on Ogden Street.
It was the Newberry's 5 & 10 and there was nobody
I'd ever known that had the exact color hair—
orange as carrots with their tops cut off—
that Mary Donahue wore.
I knocked frantically on the glass window
waved and ran around to the other side.
By the time I got to the counter her stool was empty
but warm when I pressed my hand to the vinyl.

When I came back home for Christmas break
I told my mom about Newberry's and who I'd seen.
She said she was sure I was just imagining.
You've always done that sort of thing.
Mama predicted Mary Donahue was dead
fallen into an old road works ditch
long ago on the outskirts of town
or else penniless somewhere and pregnant with two kids
washing floors in doctors' offices
and I'd never see her again.

I prefer to think differently.
Mary Donahue baked the best pies
this side of the Rockies.
It was likely she could do many other things
study literature, explore botany, write poems.
Her disposition reminded me of summer festivals
a grassy river bank with girls wading
the ones who find a secret door in the trees

converse with the moon in sign language.
I am convinced she is leading a new life
no coronation headdress maybe
but her red leather shoes lifting
even with sagebrush in them
mysterious, self-possessed
as the winds that claimed her.

Levitation

My brother said it is gross to imagine God
lifting us up out of a plague
planting us in some nebulous heaven someday.
He believed in fighting his own battles
winning the world over with triumphant hands
beating the shit out of any jackass who taunted him.

I never disclosed my imaginings to my brother after that
the way God would raise the roof of the church service
tear the heavy weighted stations of the cross
off the inside of the walls one day
let Mary have her own chapel we can worship in
how all the devout altar boys will fly away
girls by default take their place
amid the chalice, incense burners.

But in Hollis, Queens, nobody lifted off the ground
early unless it was due to cancer
a gunshot wound or old age.
My Uncle Amele was maybe the closest one
I ever saw to raise their body about six inches
above the floor.
It was Saturday.
My Aunt Bertha out grocery shopping.
Uncle had already suffered two mild strokes.
He wasn't supposed to lift heavy things
at the bakery anymore
played more cards than he once did.

I confided in him that sometimes
when the world gets too harsh
I consider flying off to heaven.
We had that kind of relationship.
He was gentle, a good listener like nobody else.
Always asked how my life was going.

Uncle said heaven was maybe a dreary place
populated by would-be sinners who
let the priest's sermons get the better.
It might be colorless as water
and then what would you do with your time there?
I said—eat. Angel food cake with no more hiss in it.
Uncle put down the pruning shears and drew me
across the yard to the hammock that swung
bodies between its metal frame.
What do you see?
Sky and sky and more sky.
Now look around the yard, what do you see?
Roses, and some yellow flowers, and your lilac bush
and my brother's stupid old cement mixer truck
and...
A lot, right?

Yes, a lot.
Could this be heaven too? he pondered.
It's not colorless and there's a lot of it.
This yard is just one thumbnail of what's out there for us.
He told me to watch closely
and he slapped his arms slowly
as if wings were coming and soon
he'd transform into a bird
but that didn't happen.
A moment later his body lifted
up off the ground.
Six inches, a foot maybe
but clearly there was grass
under his heels.
I sat amazed on the hammock.
Did I really see this?

How do you do that?
Uncle claimed he had nothing to do with it.
Don't say a word to anyone, he warned me.
They won't understand.

My Uncle Amele and I never said a peep
about what happened that afternoon.
Afterwards, my neighbor's tortillas start flying
through their open window
the little boy up the block's severed arm
begins to grow back
my mother doesn't die of heart failure
becomes the artist she was always destined to be.

As for me—
I became the girl strapped to wreckless skates
learned how to levitate
mind unruly words
the arms of the wind
in my bed.

Toni Thomas lives in Portland, Oregon. Her poems have been published in Austria, Spain, New Zealand, Canada, England, Scotland, and Australia. In the United States her work has appeared in over fifty literary magazines including *Prairie Schooner, North Dakota Quarterly, Hayden's Ferry Review, the Minnesota Review, Notre Dame Review, Poetry East*, and more. She has been twice nominated for a Pushcart prize, and won several awards. She has published nineteen collections of poetry and four books for children.

Her figurative clay sculptures have been shown in gallery exhibits in Portland and Chicago, displayed in literary magazines, and housed in private collections in the U.S. and England.

Her short documentary *One of Us* was shown at the Trans-ideology: Nostalgia festival in Berlin and at the Museum of
Contemporary Art in Taipei.

Since Toni loves to create and sits buried in reams of poems, manuscripts, clay figures and images....she likes to imagine all of them out in the world swaying wild as the lupine.

tonithomaspoetry.com

www.ingramcontent.com/pod-product-compliance
Lightning Source LLC
Chambersburg PA
CBHW031119080526
44587CB00011B/1033